Weather Report

Sunny Days

By Jennifer S. Burke

Children's Press
A Division of Grolier Publishing
New York / London / Hong Kong / Sydney
Danbury, Connecticut

Photo Credits: Cover, pp. 5, 7, 9, 11, 13, 15, 17, 19 by Angela Booth; p. 21 © Index Stock
Contributing Editor: Mark Beyer
Book Design: MaryJane Wojciechowski

Visit Children's Press on the Internet at:
http://publishing.grolier.com

Library of Congress Cataloging-in-Publication Data

Burke, Jennifer S.
   Sunny days / by Jennifer S. Burke.
     p. cm. — (Weather report)
   Includes bibliographical references and index.
   Summary: Describes various things to do for fun outdoors on sunny days.
   ISBN 0-516-23121-9 (lib. bdg.) — ISBN 0-516-23046-8 (pbk.)
   1. Outdoor recreation for children—Juvenile literature. 2. Amusements—Juvenile
literature. [1. Outdoor recreation. 2. Amusements.] I. Title.
GV191.63.B87 2000   796—dc21
                                                         00-023355

Contents

The sun is out.

It's a good day to go outside.

I wear my shorts and a tee shirt outside.

These help me to stay cool on hot, **sunny** days.

I wear **sunblock** on my arms, face, and legs.

Now my skin won't get burned by the sun.

I wear my hat.

It keeps the sun off my face.

11

On sunny days, my mom takes me to the zoo.

I like to watch the big, pink birds walk in the sun.

13

Sunny days are good days to swim.

I go swimming at the pool.

15

Sunshine helps plants to grow.

Flowers **bloom** on sunny days.

Even cold days can be sunny days.

The sun can shine **brightly** on cold days.

I wear **sunglasses** to help me see.

19

We go **sledding** on sunny winter days.

It's not so cold outside when the sun shines.

New Words

bloom (**bloom**) when a flower opens

brightly (**bryt**-lee) giving a lot of light

sledding (**sled**-ing) sliding down a hill
on a sled

sunblock (**sun**-blok) cream that
covers the skin to block sunburn

sunglasses (**sun**-glas-iz) glasses that
have dark lenses

sunny (**sun**-nee) when the sun is out
and shining

sunshine (**sun**-shyn) the bright light
from the sun

To Find Out More

Books

Cloudy Day Sunny Day
by Donald Crews
Harcourt Brace & Company

Energy From the Sun
by Allan Fowler
Children's Press

Web Sites

What is the Sun?
www.hao.ucar.edu/public/education/education.html
This site answers many questions about the sun. Find out what the sun is made of, how big it is, and other information.

Weather Gone Wild
http://tqjunior.advanced.org/5818
This site has weather topics to explore and learn about. It explains why it rains and has fun facts about the weather.

23

Index

About the Author

Jennifer S. Burke is a teacher and a writer living in New York City. She holds a master's degree in reading education from Queens College, New York.

Reading Consultants

Kris Flynn, Coordinator, Small School District Literacy, The San Diego County Office of Education

Shelly Forys, Certified Reading Recovery Specialist, W.J. Zahnow Elementary School, Waterloo, IL

Peggy McNamara, Professor, Bank Street College of Education, Reading and Literacy Program